First published in Belgium and Holland by Clavis Uitgeverij, Hasselt – Amsterdam, 2014
Copyright © 2014, Clavis Uitgeverij

English translation from the Dutch by Clavis Publishing Inc. New York
Copyright © 2015 for the English language edition: Clavis Publishing Inc. New York

Visit us on the web at www.clavisbooks.com

Mack's World of Wonder. Countries written and illustrated by Mack
Original title: *Allemaal leuke landen*
Translated from the Dutch by Clavis Publishing

ISBN 978-1-60537-248-8

This book was printed in June 2015 at Proost Industries NV, Everdongenlaan 23, 2300 Turnhout, Belgium

First Edition
10 9 8 7 6 5 4 3 2 1

Clavis Publishing supports the First Amendment and celebrates the right to read

Mack's world of WONDER

COUNTRIES

Mack

Clavis

NEW YORK

AFRICA

KENYA

In Kenya there are lots of wild animals. Ostriches, giraffes, zebras… they roam around in big national parks. People go on safari so they can see the animals in the wild. Look, this giraffe is calmly crossing the road in search of juicy leaves. The people in the car wait patiently, because in game preserves wild animals always have priority. The car can only drive on after the giraffe has reached the other side of the road.

Wild animals live on vast grasslands in Kenya. You'll find elephants, zebras, ostriches, snakes, rhinoceroses and lions! Most animals are afraid of the lions. They keep careful watch, and as soon as the lions move, the animals dash away. They don't want to end up as dinner!

Many people in Kenya live in villages or cities. But some live close to nature. They are the Masai. The Masai wander all through the country with their herds of cattle. They build their huts in one place one day, and the next week they're in another place altogether. Masai love bright colors and they wear a lot of chains around their neck. They look beautiful! They can jump very high. Can you jump too?

The marabou
is a type of stork.

Can you count
how many necklaces
this woman is wearing?

The cow sleeps
in the hut at night.

Which animal can jump highest?

EGYPT

It almost never rains in Egypt. It is usually very hot, and the ground is very dry. Most of the country is made up of huge sandy plains we call desert. In the middle of the desert are huge structures called pyramids. They were built thousands of years ago, stone by stone, without the help of modern machines! Isn't that amazing?

Sphinx.

Sun.

Water.

Cry, fly, sail, walk.

This crocodile is almost a mummy!

The kings of ancient Egypt, called Pharaohs, were buried in the pyramids. They were mummified after their death – which means they were wrapped up in cloth. Their pets were too! Near the pyramids is a big statue with the body of a lion and the head of a human being: the sphinx. Did you know that ancient Egyptian writing is made of pictures not letters? The pictures are called hieroglyphs. Can you tell what is written in the stones?

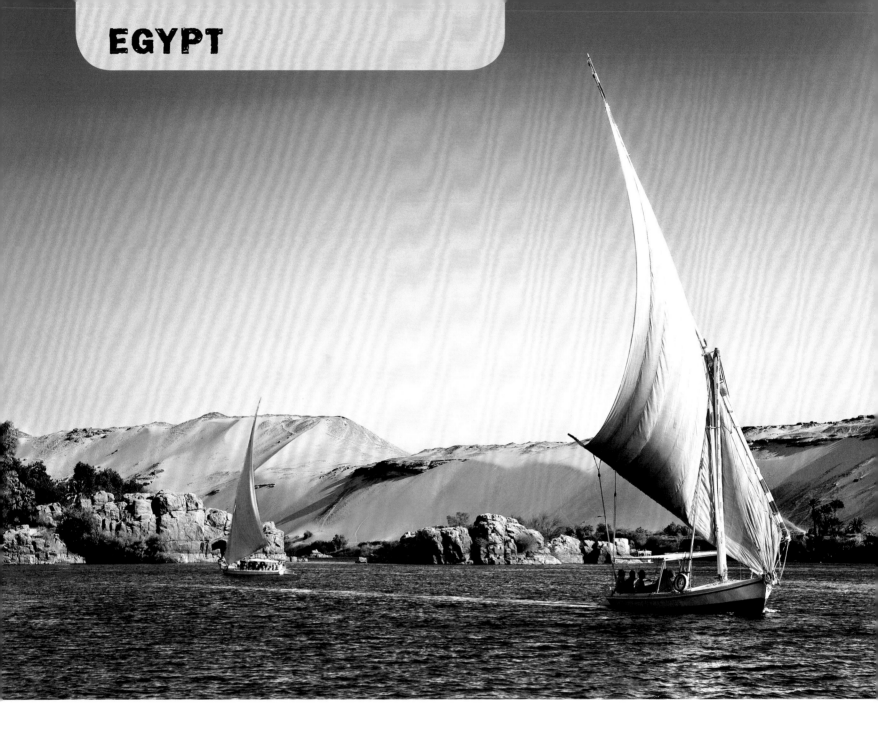

The Nile river flows through Egypt. Because it almost never rains in Egypt, it's hard for trees and plants to grow. But many plants grow on the banks of the Nile, and that's where most Egyptians live. Some people also live in the dry deserts! They mostly sleep in tents and protect themselves against the sand and hot sun by wearing long clothes and headscarves.

Did you know that you sometimes find water and trees in the middle of the desert? That's called an oasis.

Camels don't mind dry weather. They store fat in their lumps so they can go for a long time without eating or drinking.

What animal is standing in the sandstorm?

MOROCCO

In Morocco you find green palm trees, deserts and a lot of mountains. On one of those mountains there is a special city that is surrounded by big walls and even bigger towers. The city is built out of beautiful pink-orange-red colored sandstone. The beautiful houses are famous all over the world.

Black ibis.

Koutoubia mosque.

In the middle of the marketplace in Marrakesh there is a high tower. It's the tower of the Koutoubia mosque. When it's time for Muslim Moroccans to pray, an Arabic call sounds from the tower. Then everybody knows it's time for the prayers to start. Beautiful birds, like the rare black ibis, circle around the tower. Moroccans love tea. They drink honey-sweetened tea from colored glasses. Yummy!

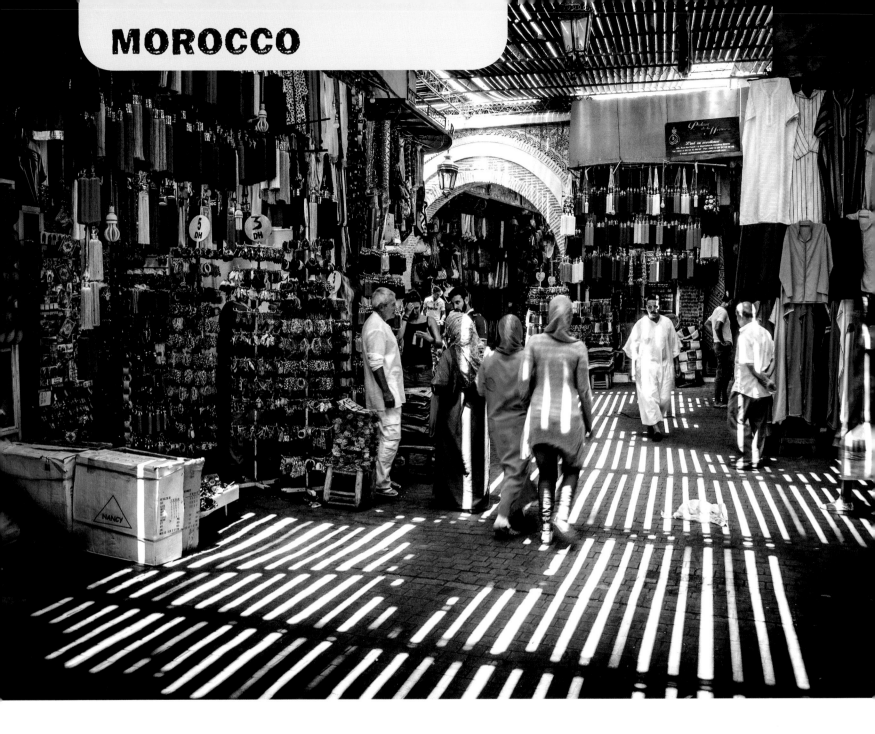

MOROCCO

In almost every Moroccan city you'll find a wonderful market called a souk. The souk in Marrakesh might be the biggest market in Africa. People come to this market to buy clothes and food and even carpets. The things that are for sale don't have a fixed price, you have to bargain with the salesman. It's like a game. There are many things to see and do in a souk. People make music and you can feast on delicious tea and snacks.

You can find fresh vegetables and fruit at the market.

The goats in Morocco love climbing. Sometimes they even climb trees!

Which one is the Moroccan shoe?

America

UNITED STATES

The United States of America is one of the biggest countries in the world. New York City is the biggest city in the United States. You can see the skyline from far away. That's because the buildings are so high. They're called skyscrapers because they seem to touch the sky. Luckily you don't have to climb the stairs to get to the top of a skyscraper. There are superfast elevators that take you to the highest floors.

The Empire State Building.

The Statue of Liberty.

A yellow New York taxi.

It's always very busy in New York. Traffic is on the go day
and night. A woman carrying a torch welcomes visitors to New York.
Not a real woman, of course, a statue! The statue is called the Statue
of Liberty. She stands on a small island and she is so big that people
can stand in her crown! The Empire State Building is another famous
building in New York. It was the first skyscraper, and has more than one
hundred floors. Do you know what food Americans love? Hamburgers!

UNITED STATES

The United States has lots of big cities, but it's not made up only of big cities. There are beautiful nature reserves too. One of the best known is Monument Valley. In a bare, earth-colored landscape you suddenly see these peculiar rocks. They are as big as a castle – or actually as big as five castles together. The rocks are many different shapes. One looks like a church, the other like a tower.

Careful! There are buffalos and brown bears too. And eagles that fly in the air.

In Yellowstone National Park you find springs that are bright blue. So pretty!

Walt Disney was an American, he made cartoons and the characters on these stamps. Do you recognize them?

MEXICO

Mexico is a country full of color and music. On the cozy squares you can sometimes hear the music of the mariachi. The musicians wear traditional clothes and big hats. The hat with its broad brim is called a sombrero. Women in colorful skirts dance to the music of the mariachi. They move their bodies and arms so their skirts move like waves in the ocean.

If you wear a sombrero on your head, your face will always be in the shade.

This Mexican is taking a nap in a hammock.

Mexicans love music and good food. Have you ever tasted Mexican food, like tacos or tortillas which are filled with beans, corn, guacamole and hot peppers. Those peppers are spicy and burn your mouth if you're not careful! Did you know that chocolate originally comes from Mexico? You can drink delicious hot chocolate in Mexico. With spicy chili pepper!

MEXICO

Mexico has many different landscapes. There are deserts with big cactuses, beautiful bays, white beaches, and high mountains as well as tropical forests. There are old temples hidden in the forests and mountains. The Aztecs built the temples a long time ago. The Aztecs were very smart. They dug canals, invented a calendar, and wrote books. And they built beautiful temples for their gods.

Aztecs also made beautiful totem poles.

The masked Zorro was a Mexican.

WANTED

A giant cactus.

The roadrunner is real. It lives in Mexico!

Which hat is a Mexican sombrero?

BRAZIL

Brazil is a very big country. The best-known city is Rio de Janeiro. The city overlooks the ocean. Inhabitants of Rio can walk to the famous Copacabana beach, or to one of the other beautiful white beaches. The warm beaches are full of life. In Brazil you hear cheerful music all the time. And you see people playing soccer everywhere. Some soccer players do amazing things with the ball. A lot of famous soccer players were born in Brazil!

The Brazilians love dancing, especially during carnival. Carnival in
Rio is famous all over the world. Nowhere else is carnival celebrated by
as many people as it is in Rio de Janeiro. People work on their
costumes for months. They use feathers, glitter and diamonds.
For days and nights the whole city dances the samba in the streets.
Children play along using pans and wooden spoons.

BRAZIL

The Amazon, which is the biggest tropical rainforest in the world, is in Brazil. In the Amazon it is always very warm and damp. Monkeys use vines to swing from branch to branch, and the air is filled with the sounds of croaking frogs and growling panthers. There are also some Indian tribes who live in the forest. They hunt with bows and arrows. They understand all the plants and know exactly which ones they can use to heal them when they get sick.

The inhabitants of the Amazon:

parrots

toucan

jaguar

monkey

piranhas

Which animals are hiding behind the vines?

GREENLAND

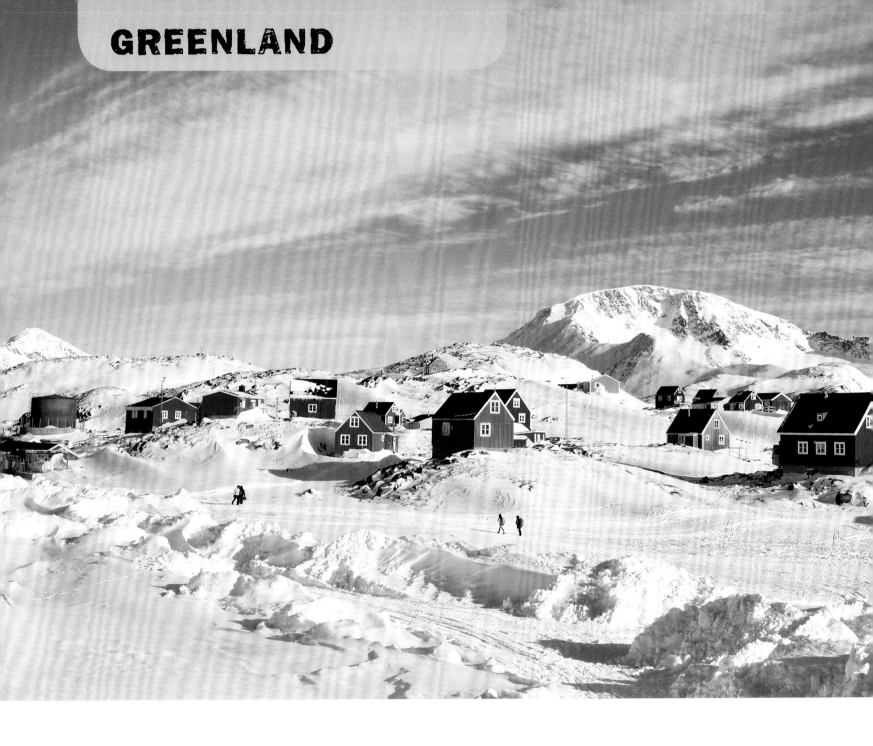

Greenland isn't green, it's white! That's because there is almost always snow on the ground. Greenland is one of the coldest countries in the world. If you want to drink a glass of water in Greenland, you have to do it really quickly or else the water freezes! In the middle of all that snow there are a few colorful houses. That's where the Greenlanders live. The Inuit or Eskimos were the first inhabitants of Greenland. Many Inuit still live there!

A dog sled is sometimes even more useful than a car in Greenland. Cars slip and slide in the snow, but snow doesn't bother strong dogs. Do you see all those beautiful colors in the sky? It looks as if the sky is dancing. Those are the polar lights or northern lights. The inhabitants of Greenland can look at them for hours and hours. Some people come from the other side of the world just to see the beautiful light show.

The animals in Greenland - like seals, reindeer, and snowy owls - are able to live in very cold weather. With their soft white fur, polar bears look like cuddly toys. But you'd better not try and cuddle them, because polar bears are dangerous. The inhabitants of Greenland carefully close their doors before they go to sleep. They don't want to wake up to a polar bear in their houses!

The inhabitants of Greenland:

arctic wolf

snow owl

reindeer

arctic hare

seals

Do you know these animals? Although they love the cold, they don't live in Greenland, they live on the South Pole. Greenland is near the North Pole!

EUROPE

ITALY

Italy is filled with beautiful old cities. One of the most interesting is Venice, a city built on the water. There are no highways in Venice, but there are rivers and canals. There are no cars, but there are lots of boats called gondolas. If you want to go to the bakery, you just get in a gondola. Gondolas are like water taxis. If you are lucky, the gondolier will sing for you as he paddles you around! *Oh, mamma mia!*

MAMMA MIA

Rome is the capital of Italy. When you walk through the center of Rome, you see remains of old buildings everywhere. The ancient Romans built the buildings a very long time ago, and sometimes there is quite a lot of the building left. These are the ruins of the Coliseum, an arena where men fought with dangerous lions and tigers. And do you see the Tower of Pisa? It is leaning. Do you think it will fall?

In Italy you find all kinds of good food. Delicious ice cream, coffee, pizza and… pasta! Have you ever eaten spaghetti? It tastes good, doesn't it? But it can also be difficult to eat. Italians twirl the long strands of pasta into a ball using their forks and spoons. It's much easier to eat that way! You have to get just the right amount of spaghetti though. Too many strands make a ball that is too big to eat!

In the Italian town
of Portofino the
houses are painted
in cheerful colors.

Did you know that
Pinocchio comes
from Italy?

Which pizzas are exactly the same?

ENGLAND

England is a huge island. It is totally surrounded by water. London is the biggest city. The buses in London are red. They are called double decker buses, because they have two levels. You can sit below or on top. You get in, buy a ticket from the driver, and then climb a few steps to the top level. If you sit in front you'll have a spectacular view of all sorts of interesting buildings.

Buckingham Palace.

uards.

The queen of England lives in Buckingham Palace in
London. There are guards in front of the palace gates. They wear a
uniform with black trousers and a red jacket. They wear tall fuzzy hats
on their heads. The guards stand stiff as rods for hours and hours –
even when it rains. They are not allowed to move at all. They're not
even allowed to smile! A few times a day new guards arrive, then there
is a ceremony called the Changing of the Guard.

In England there are a lot of old castles. Some castles are in ruins, but other castles are almost entirely preserved. You can see the towers, moats, and big drawbridges. Can you imagine brave knights fighting with swords in the inner court? Maybe they are fighting for a princess who is locked in the tower?

An English village.

How many sheep do you count in the circle of stones?

FRANCE

The capital of France is Paris. In the centre of Paris there is a tall tower. You can't miss it – it's called the Eiffel Tower! From the top of the Eiffel Tower you can see the whole city. Paris is often called The City of Lights, and when you look at the city from the tower at night you can see why. It's so pretty! There are many tall buildings in Paris, but none are as tall as the Eiffel Tower. Maybe that is why it is so famous.

Place du Tertre, in Montmartre, is a cozy square!

The buildings in Paris are all very old. One of the most famous is the Cathedral of Notre Dame de Paris. There is a lot to see and do in the city. In the neighborhood called Montmartre, artists gather to paint portraits and landscapes. They also draw the monuments in Paris. Do you see the Eiffel Tower?

FRANCE

In the South of France, in summer, the sun shines almost every day. And, of course, sunflowers love the sun! You find beautiful fields of sunflowers on the French countryside. People in France love the sun and good food, so they love eating outside. You can have a scrumptious French picnic with baguettes, croissants, cheese and wine. *Bon appétit!*

A delicious French picnic!

Do you see the French croissant?

Russia is the biggest country in the world. There are a lot of huge lakes, rivers and woods in Russia. And a lot of people live in Russia. Russians love dance. Russian ballets are famous around the world. Do you know *The Nutcracker*? In that story a nutcracker comes to life. Together with a girl and a Sugar Plum Fairy he travels through a few countries. Every country has its own music and its own dance. It's beautiful!

Saint Basil's Cathedral.

Russians are real space travelers.

Red Square.

Moscow is the capital of Russia. The center of this huge city is the Red Square. There are beautiful buildings around the square, but the prettiest one might be Saint Basil's Cathedral. It looks like a castle from a fairy tale with all those beautiful turrets! Did you know the first human in space was a Russian?

In winter it's not just a little cold in Russia, it's awfully cold.
It freezes almost every day. The Russians put on warm fur caps to keep
themselves warm. But horses don't mind the cold and snow. They don't slip
on slippery roads. It's fun to drive around in a troika, a handy sled pulled
by three horses.

In winter Russia looks like a fairy tale.

The balalaika is a triangle shaped stringed instrument.

Which Russian doll or matryoshka is the smallest? Which is the largest?

Asia

CHINA

More people live in China than in any other country in the world. Some Chinese live in small houses in the countryside, others live in ultramodern apartments in the city. Several of the highest skyscrapers in the world are in China. So, is China very modern? Yes, but Chinese people are very proud of their ancient history too. Look at this old ship sailing in Hong Kong's modern harbor. You find old and new side by side in China.

Chinese characters.

Dragons are thought of as lucky in China. That is why you see
fire-breathing dragons everywhere – in restaurants
and houses, on palace walls and gates, in stores and on
clothing. Most dragons are brightly colored or covered with
a thin layer of gold. Chinese like the cheerful color red. That is why
traditional Chinese clothes are often red.

The most famous wall in the world is in China. The Great
Wall of China was built thousands of years ago to keep enemies away.
Today a lot of tourists come to walk on the wall. But they can't walk along
the whole wall, because the wall is over thirteen thousand miles long!
It is so long that astronauts can see it from space.

Chinese love rice.
Rice plants grow in fields called paddies.

The kite was
invented
in China.

Pandas live in China.
They eat bamboo all day long!

The giant panda is bigger than the red panda. Do you see the difference?

INDONESIA

Indonesia is a warm country. Very warm. The sun is always high in the sky. But it rains often too. Children in Indonesia often have to shelter underneath a sort of umbrella they make from the leaves of a banana tree. Under the leaves they are protected from the bright sun and the wet rain. That's smart!

The inhabitants of the jungle of Indonesia:

orang-utan

hornbill

tiger

rafflesia

A lot of wild animals live in the jungles of Indonesia: funny orang-utans, beautiful hornbills, and dangerous tigers. The biggest flower in the world also grows in the jungles of Indonesia. It's called the rafflesia. The rafflesia is bigger than five pizzas together and blooms only now and then. When it does, you can smell it. Because the rafflesia smells very bad… like rotten meat! All animals run away from it. Except for flies – they love the rafflesia.

INDONESIA

Indonesia is made of hundreds of tiny islands. One of those islands is beautiful Bali. On Bali you find wonderful old temples. The Balinese often dance and sing in the temples. And they put out dishes with delicious food and colorful flowers as offerings. This big Elephant Cave was built as a temple. It is more than one thousand years old!

The rice fields
of Indonesia look like
a flight of stairs.

Balinese dancers put on
beautiful masks.

The Borobudur is one
of the most famous temples
in the world.

On the island of Sumatra the houses have peaked roofs. Which roof has the most peaks?

In India you'll find the long river Ganges. Many people in India believe the Ganges is a holy river. Every year millions of people go there to bathe in the river and to clean their bodies and their spirits. Some people wash their clothes in the river, others empty their garbage into it! The Ganges may be a holy river, but it's not very clean.

Fakir on a bed of nails.

Gate of Palace Mysore.

When there is something to celebrate in India

people wear long robes and strings of beads. They also decorate their hands with all sorts of patterns. It looks lovely! A lot of people in India believe you can do anything. Even when other people think it is impossible. A fakir is a sort of magician who can really do anything. On top of this gate to the Palace Mysore a fakir is lying down on a bed of nails. Ouch! Do you think it hurts?

INDIA

In India you can visit the Taj Mahal, one of the most beautiful buildings in the world. The Taj Mahal is made of white marble. The big building looks a little like a church or a mosque, but it's actually a tomb. A very big tomb. A long time ago the emperor Shah Jahan ordered it built for his wife who died. He loved her very much. They say that in the month after his wife died, Shah Jahan's beard grew as light as the Taj Mahal's white marble from grief.

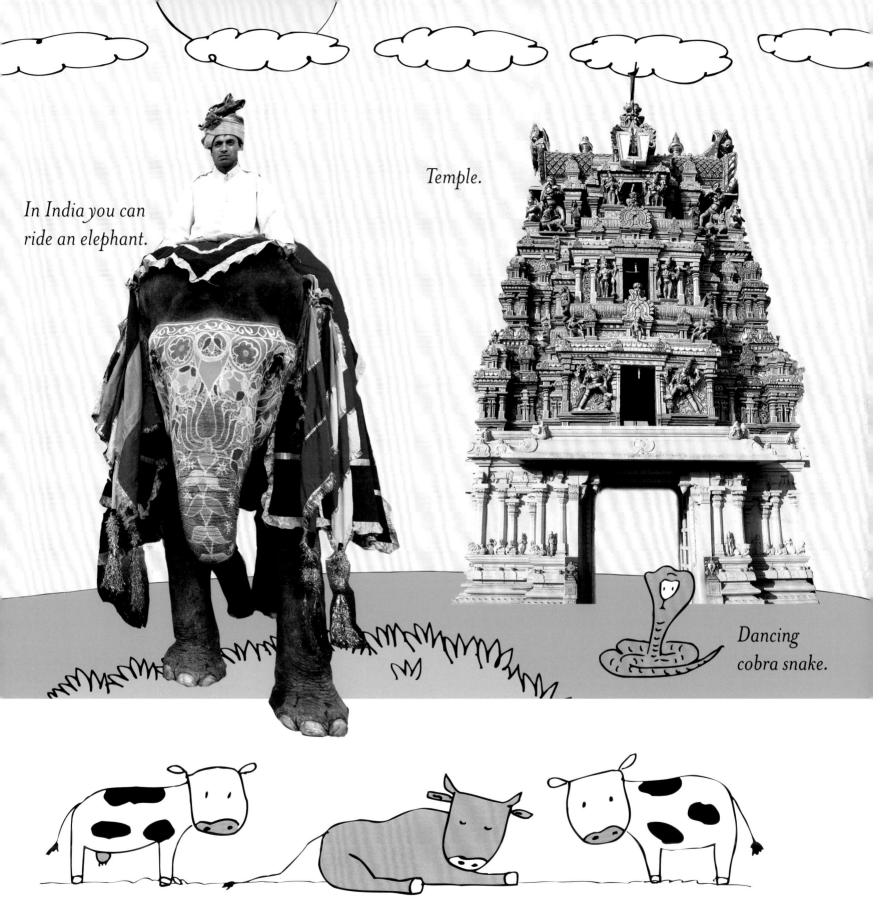

In India you can ride an elephant.

Temple.

Dancing cobra snake.

In India cows are holy. They don't have to do anything.
Which cow do you think is tired?

JAPAN

Japan consists of a lot of small islands. On those islands there are big cities. Tokyo, the capital of Japan, is very big. Millions and millions of people live in Tokyo. More than in some countries! Japanese people love to sing, especially karaoke. They read the lyrics to a song on a screen and then they sing along.

Japanese common crane.

The holy Fuji Volcano.

Outside the cities you find high mountains and beautiful gardens. Japanese gardens are so pretty they are copied in other countries. Between the colorful flowers and the calm greenery, there are small temples called pagodas. Bonsai trees are also found in Japan. The trees are clipped so they stay very, very small.

JAPAN

Some Japanese people sit happily on a pillow or on a straw carpet on the floor to eat. They don't use a knife and fork, they eat with chopsticks. That's not easy! Geishas are traditional Japanese hostesses. They have black hair, beautiful painted mouths, and white faces. It looks as if they are wearing masks.

The Japanese common crane can dance really beautifully.

Japanese girl in a traditional kimono.

The Japanese eat rice with chopsticks.

Which Japanese sumo wrestler is a little afraid?

AUSTRALIA

AUSTRALIA

Australia is very big, but not that many people live there. Neighbors sometimes live a few miles apart. Australians love sports. Tennis, swimming and… surfing! Australia has beautiful beaches and high waves. And you need those to surf. The bigger the wave, the more fun it is for surfers.

*Throw a boomerang
and it comes back all by itself!*

The red Uluru rock.

In Australia there are a lot of interesting animals. Although not all of them walk! Kangaroos move around by hopping. Here you see two kangaroos near the red Uluru rock. If you take a good look, you can see a baby kangaroo in its mother's pouch. Fluffy koala bears also live in Australia – they climb high up in eucalyptus trees. Did you know that the boomerang comes from Australia? If you throw a boomerang, it turns around and flies right back! To do it right though, you have to practice a lot.

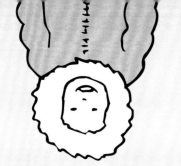